T0418260

**The Teen Guide to Adulting:
Gaining Financial Independence**

What You Need to Know About

JOB SEARCHING

ALEXIS BURLING

New York

Published in 2021 by The Rosen Publishing Group, Inc.
29 East 21st Street, New York, NY 10010

First Edition

Library of Congress Cataloging-in-Publication Data

Names: Burling, Alexis, author.
Title: What you need to know about job searching / Alexis Burling.
Description: First edition. | New York : Rosen Publishing, 2021. | Series:
The teen guide to adulting : gaining financial independence | Includes
bibliographical references and index. | Audience: Grades 7-12.
Identifiers: LCCN 2019013734 | ISBN 9781725340602 (library
binding) | ISBN 9781725340596 (paperback)
Subjects: LCSH: Job hunting—Juvenile literature. | Résumés (Employment)—
Juvenile literature. | Employment interviewing—Juvenile literature. |
Teenagers—Vocational guidance—Juvenile literature.
Classification: LCC HF5382.7 .B875 2021 | DDC 650.14—dc23
LC record available at https://lccn.loc.gov/2019013734

Manufactured in China

CONTENTS

INTRODUCTION

When Hayley Hanway graduated from the University of Michigan in the summer of 2013, she thought her job search would be a breeze. She had majored in environmental science at one of the best public universities in the United States. Her grade point average had been consistently good. She had completed a prestigious climate science program at Oxford University in England and had even spent a summer doing environmental conservation work in New Zealand.

Given her stellar college experience, Hanway thought job recruiters would be lining up to hire her. But instead of landing her dream job, she spent months sending in applications and getting rejections or no responses in return. After nearly six months of looking, she took a part-time position at a Macy's fragrance counter. Because she was offered only minimum wage, she couldn't even afford to pay rent on a shared apartment. With no other options available to her, she moved into her parents' basement.

In April 2014, Hanway was offered a job in her field as a lead horticulturist at a nearby zoo. The position promised paid vacation time and health benefits. But the wage was a measly $12 an hour, which meant she still couldn't afford to live on her own. She went back to school to get her master's degree in environmental management, but even that didn't help matters much. After graduation, she applied for forty jobs, but got called for only four interviews. Finally, in September

Researching jobs, finding suitable companies, and creating a sharp résumé is incredibly time-consuming work. Sometimes it can take a while—and a lot of rejections—to pay off.

2018, she was offered what she considered to be the perfect position—as a science writer for Duke University—and it paid well to boot. She accepted.

Hanway's postcollege situation might sound demoralizing, but it's not unique. According to the National Center for Family and Marriage Research at Bowling Green State University, 23 percent of people ages twenty-five to twenty-nine lived with their parents or guardians in 2018—up from 17 percent a decade earlier—due to college loans, difficulty finding work, or low-paying first jobs. What's more, a 2017 study by Strada Education Network and Gallup, which surveyed 32,000 students across 43 four-year institutions, found that a majority of college students felt overwhelmed and underprepared when navigating a job search postgraduation. A mere third of them believed they had the necessary skills required to succeed or advance in the workplace. Only half thought their choice of major might actually pave the way to a decent job.

This prognosis seems daunting. But there is a silver lining. According to the *New York Times*, the unemployment rate for bachelor's degree recipients ages twenty to twenty-nine is at 8.3 percent—the lowest it's been since 2007. That means there *are* jobs out there for young people. They just have to know where to look and have the know-how and willpower to get them.

Landing a job takes skill and persistence. But knowing what information to put on a résumé, how to write a polished cover letter, and how to act professional in a job interview will put you ahead of the game. Being aware of what to do after the interview takes place, including why thank-you notes are important, is essential, too. Searching for a job can be stressful at any age, especially if you're just starting out. But when armed with the right tools and a bit of confidence, you'll be well on your way to building a fulfilling career.

CHAPTER ONE

FINDING YOUR PASSION

Kelly Williams Brown is in her mid-thirties and knows a little something about becoming an adult. She's the author of the book *Adulting: How to Become a Grown-Up in 535 Easy(ish) Steps*. Since its publication in 2018, the quirky guide has become so popular with young people that it has gone on to become a bestseller.

But Brown wasn't always an expert on how to ease into adulthood with panache. She spent years fumbling around—and more than once failed miserably at whatever she was trying to accomplish. Prior to becoming a freelance writer, Brown had many different jobs. She was a cocktail waitress on Bourbon Street in New Orleans, Louisiana. She also worked as a copywriter and a news reporter at a newspaper.

According to Brown, one of the most essential things about being a responsible grownup is having a job. She also insists there's more than one "perfect" job for each person. "Often, we decide that it is this *one job* or *one industry* that will make us happy," she writes in *Adulting*. "The truth is that you could do really well and find satisfaction with lots of different types of jobs, including some that you may never, ever have considered."

So how do you find a killer job or even a few different possibilities that might be right for you? Once you land on some ideas, what are some of the skills you'll need to perform the work successfully? To jumpstart your journey to crafting a rewarding career, it's important to first think about what you like to do—and what you're good at.

KNOW YOUR SKILLS

Figuring out what you want to do for a lifelong career—or even for a summer job—can seem like an insurmountable task. But the first step is actually quite simple (and fun!). According to career counselor Carol Christen, the easiest way to narrow down a seemingly endless list of potential careers is to conceptualize your job search within the context of your interests.

"Your interests can lead you in many different directions for your work life," Christen writes in *What Color Is Your Parachute? For Teens*. "It's true that interests change with time, age, and exposure to new people, places, and experiences. But it's also true that your interests now may be with you all your life, so naming your current interests is a great starting place for finding work you'll love.

Once you have a firm grasp of what you like to do, it's then important to determine whether you have the skills (or the desire) required to pursue that type of work full time. For example, maybe you're obsessed with playing video games. A long-term career smacking baddies in the latest *Assassin's Creed* or Marvel's *Spider-Man* is probably unlikely. But a video game designer? That might be in your wheelhouse as long as you learn some necessary skills for the job, such as computer programming or animation.

The golden rule when thinking about finding work is to distinguish whether something is merely a hobby or a passion that can be turned into a career using your skill set. With Christen's advice in mind, try this simple exercise: make a list of all your interests. Then write down all of your skills in a second column. Be honest and thorough! Now look both

During the job search, making lists is a smart way to get your head clear and priorities in order. Plus, crossing off items on a to-do list feels very rewarding.

lists over to make sure you've written down *everything* you're good at. Even the seemingly smallest skill—like keeping track of dates and passwords—can be useful in a future career.

DEVELOP AN ACTION PLAN

Once you've developed your list, see if you can combine any of your interests and skills to come up with potential job options. If you're drawing a blank, try doing an internet search to see which career paths or positions might fit with your list, then dig a little deeper. A great place to start is the *Occupational Outlook Handbook* (https://www.bls.gov/ooh). It's a meticulously researched and up-to-date resource from the US Department of Labor's Bureau of Labor Statistics (BLS) that provides information about what various workers do on the job, working conditions, required training and education, earnings, and expected job prospects. You can search different types of careers according to the median pay, entry-level education required, number of new jobs, on-the-job training opportunities, or projected growth rate in the field.

For example, if you are thinking about a career in health care, there are a number of paths you can take. Opticians help customers decide which eyeglass frames or contact lenses to buy. They also assist doctors, either ophthalmologists or optometrists, with tasks around the clinic. To become an optician, you would need a high school diploma or the equivalent. According to a September 2018 BLS report, opticians make, on average, $36,250 a year.

If you wanted to work toward becoming an optometrist, you would have to go to college and then optometry school to get your doctor of optometry degree. But the good news is that both opticians and optometrists are in high demand. According to the BLS's September 2018 report, the job outlook for opticians and optometrists is a 15 percent and 18 percent growth rate respectively, which is much faster than average.

Many high schools have a career coach or guidance counselor on staff who can help you pinpoint your strengths and weaknesses or even chart a path to rewarding employment options.

In addition to doing online research, take control of your job search by talking to your school's guidance counselor or sign on with an independent career counselor. He or she will likely have lots of positive, relevant tips on how to move forward and set realistic goals. These types of job-focused counselors can recommend career-related books to check out of the library, such as Carol Christen's book. They are also excellent at helping you stay motivated and on track during your journey.

THE GIG ECONOMY

When you're first starting out in your job search, you'll most likely be researching options for full-time employment. In a lot of cases, a full-time job comes with a regular, dependable salary, health benefits, and a structured routine. But there's also another option: becoming your own boss and freelancing for different clients.

This type of worker is part of what's known as the gig economy. That's a buzzy term used to describe the segment of the job market in which temporary or contract positions are the norm. Instead of hiring workers full time and covering their benefits, organizations develop contracts with independent workers for short-term engagements instead.

These days, the gig economy is booming. In 2018, the BLS reported that fifty-five million people in the United States were "gig workers." That's more than 35 percent of the US workforce. Due to the instability of the traditional workforce model, as well as increasingly accessible technology that makes working

LIVING THE GIG ECONOMY LIFESTYLE

In 2018, Jada Yuan landed what many people would consider to be a dream gig. Out of 13,000 applicants, she was hired by the *New York Times* to visit 52 exotic places around the world and write about them for the paper. Over the course of a year, her itinerary included swimming in waterfalls in Australia and paragliding off mountaintops in Switzerland. Though Yuan wasn't technically on staff at the paper, the *Times* did pay her for every article she submitted. They also paid for her travel expenses and meals.

Not everyone has the wherewithal, skills, or frankly the luck that Yuan had when being chosen for her ongoing assignment. But there are plenty of other excellent gig jobs available. Some examples include musician, copywriter, mechanic, coder, app developer, carpenter, and, yes, travel blogger.

Jada Yuan makes an appearance during Vulture Festival LA 2017 in Hollywood, California.

remotely seamless and easier, the number is projected to jump to 43 percent by 2020.

Of course, there are many downsides to freelancing full time. Gig workers don't get health insurance from their employers, so they need to find some on their own, which can be expensive. A steady paycheck is nearly unheard of, unless it's being paid out by a long-term client. Other downsides include having to keep track of projected income for yearly

Freelancers have the flexibility to decide when and where to work. They can even catch up on business emails while visiting a tropical rainforest!

taxes and a general lack of social interaction in the workplace (if the workplace is home).

But there are benefits to being your own boss. Gig workers make their own schedules. That means they can go on vacation whenever they want—as long as they have the time and money. They have the freedom to accept or decline job offers, something that might not be possible in a regular job. Perhaps the neatest perk about being a freelancer is being able to work whenever—and wherever—you want. If there's an internet connection and you have the necessary tools, you could feasibly work on an assignment while on the beach in Tahiti!

"Fifty years ago, you'd land your first (and often last) job at a stable company, clock in and out for several decades, and then retire," says Peter Swaniker, founder and chief executive officer (CEO) of Ximble, in *Forbes* magazine. "But young people today go into the workforce knowing that their career will likely be in flux. They have to be prepared to keep learning and anticipating trends so they don't find themselves unexpectedly out of work … The pace of change in the global workforce is accelerating. To succeed, we have to adapt just as quickly."

MYTHS & FACTS

MYTH   **There is one job out there for everyone, and all you have to do is find it.**

Fact   *There are many different types of jobs that are suitable for each person at different points in life. Just make sure you know or can learn the necessary skills for the job you're considering.*

MYTH   **Changing jobs often is frowned upon by prospective employers.**

Fact   *While flitting from job to job can be a red flag, it's not a reason to dismiss a potential job applicant. Common practice is to stay at a job for at least a year before bailing so you can get a sense of what the job is about and gain valuable experience you may be able to use elsewhere.*

MYTH   **Switching careers is impossible.**

Fact   *As the economy continues to change and evolve, transferring between careers has become possible—and more common. Sometimes pursuing an alternate career can just mean getting more education or training.*

CHAPTER TWO

CRAFTING A SUPERSTAR RÉSUMÉ

Congratulations on figuring out a few career paths that might be suitable for you. The next step is putting together a résumé to send to a potential employer. Your résumé is a summary of your education, professional experience, skills, and goals presented in one neatly organized document.

According to job search website CareerBuilder, companies receive more than seventy-five résumés, on average, for each of their open positions. Thirty-eight percent of human resources managers report that they spend just one to two minutes reviewing each application they receive—and that includes the cover letter. Seventeen percent spend less than one minute.

Aside from printing out your résumé on fluorescent pink paper (which is never a good idea), standing out in such a crowded applicant pool might seem difficult. But instead of giving up before you've even begun, give yourself the challenge to create a superstar résumé. And remember, says Rosemary Haefner, vice president of human resources at CareerBuilder, "human resources managers serve on the front lines of a company's recruitment efforts and are often the gatekeepers of the interview process. Because they can

According to a Glassdoor report, each corporate job listing attracts 250 résumés on average, but only four to six people will get an interview. Make sure your résumé stands out.

receive a large volume of applications, you [only] have a matter of seconds to make a lasting impression."

A word to the wise before you begin: crafting a killer résumé that best reflects your capabilities and attracts hiring managers' attention isn't a quick process, nor should it be. It takes patience and a willingness to revise, revise, and revise some more to get the job done. But that's normal. After all, it took you a long time to acquire the skills you have. Don't rush getting it all down on paper just to get this part of the job-search journey over with.

GO CHRONOLOGICAL

According to Martin Yate, author of *Knock 'em Dead: The Ultimate Job Search Guide*, a good résumé "establishes an achievable goal for your search, opens the doors of opportunity for interviews, prepares you for the questions interviewers will ask, and acts as a powerful ambassador at decision time." It needs to stand out from dozens of other résumés and create a stellar impression while also being professional. It should also present your relevant skills and qualities in a clear, concise manner.

There are many ways to structure a résumé depending on the field you're in. Before beginning this process, do some initial research at the library or online about what types of résumés are required for the types of jobs you're looking for. Artists, musicians, or those who work in a creative industry, for example, might use what's called a functional résumé. It focuses on your skills and abilities rather than your work history.

For a majority of fields, the chronological résumé is the way to go. It lists your current or most recent job first, then works backward, listing previously held jobs underneath. If you're just starting out in your career, internships are also acceptable to include. Each listing should state the job title, the name and location of the employer, and the length of time you served in the position. List two or three bullet points describing your top achievements underneath.

"Don't try to put every detail of your background into your [résumé]," warns Lynn Williams, author of *Ultimate Job Search: Master the Art of Finding Your Ideal Job, Getting an Interview and Networking*. "Put in what will interest an employer and make him or her want to know more about you. The things employers most want to know are whether you have the specific skills needed for the job; the right sort of experience; an understanding of what the job requires; [and] the personal qualities needed."

Depending on how you decide to format your résumé, another section should list pertinent skills such as your knowledge of graphic design programs like Adobe Photoshop or content management systems like WordPress. If you're proficient or fluent in a foreign language, that's something to mention here, too.

A third section describes your education credentials. Professionals often list where they completed college and whether or not they attended graduate school. They also list the name of their degree and the date they graduated, as well as any other career-related courses they've taken. If you're still in high school or are looking for jobs as an undergraduate student, this section is sometimes listed at the top of your résumé before your professional experience.

Finally, if you have enough room on the page, some other important information to include is a list of awards you received either at school or throughout your career. Memberships in important industry-related clubs or associations are helpful to note, as well as any volunteering experience you might have. As with everything you choose to include on your résumé, make sure it's relevant. While you might love baking cookies every Sunday, that pastime most likely won't get you hired.

CARRIE GALLAGHER

1809 Ellison Creek Rd.• Clemmons, NC 27012 • (919) 945 3595 • cagallagher@gmail.com • www.carriegallagher.com

Creative and driven honor roll high school graduate with a passion for writing, editing, blogging, and journalism. Four years' experience managing a high school newsroom. Excellent communications skills and reliable with deadlines.

EDUCATION
Weston High School (2015–2019)
- High School Diploma (GPA 3.83); Member of National Honor Society

Medill-Northwestern Journalism Institute (July 2018)
- Program for high school students interested in becoming writers and editors for print, online and broadcast

PROFESSIONAL EXPERIENCE
Editorial Intern at Rosen Publishing
New York, NY • June 2019 to September 2019
- Assisted editors in project planning and creating marketing materials for ALA and NCTE publishing conferences
- Handled submissions slush pile; read manuscripts for interest, clarity, and style
- Helped shaped the company's social media presence by managing its Twitter, Facebook, and Instagram feeds

Editor at Weston High News
Clemmons, NC • September 2016 to June 2019
- Curated and managed all aspects of creating a bi-weekly high school newspaper, including reviewing submissions; curating and writing content; line-editing layouts; maintaining in-house editorial, art, and production schedules; promoting articles on social media platforms
- Worked with local businesses to secure advertisements, saving the school 25 percent in production costs

Office Assistant at Winston-Salem Journal
Winston-Salem, NC • June 2017 to September 2017
- Shadowed reporters and did some light reporting and fact-checking
- Assisted newsroom staff in administrative duties, such as filing, data entry, mail distribution, ordering office supplies, and processing invoices

VOLUNTEER EXPERIENCE
- Candy Striper at Piedmont Children's Hospital (2018–2019)
- Care Assistant at The Humane Society (2015–2017), Georgetown Animal Hospital (2014)

AWARDS
- 2019 Scholastic Pacemaker Award (for Journalism)
- 2019 Harvard Book Award
- 2018 Scholastic Writing Award
- National Honor Society

TECHNICAL SKILLS
- MS Office Suite; Adobe Creative Suite, Photoshop; WordPress, Squarespace; Social Media Platforms; PC and Mac
- Fluent in Spanish; Proficient in French; Learning Chinese

Résumés come in many different shapes and forms. This is an example of a chronological résumé that a student might send out after graduating from high school.

THE LOWDOWN ON REFERENCES

A key part of the job-search process is providing your recruiter or hiring manager with references. Your references are three to five professional contacts who can vouch for your skills and abilities, like a former internship or volunteer program supervisor—not your best friend or mother. If you're applying for a job using an online form, some applications ask for a list of references right off the bat during the submission process. Other times, you can just provide a potential employer with the names during the interview or in a follow-up message. A third option is that some employers may ask that your references submit letters of recommendation, also known as reference letters. Whatever the case may be, it's important to prepare your

References are an integral part of the job application process. Start by asking bosses or colleagues you've worked with who can vouch for your skills and expertise.

your list of references in advance. The list should include each individual's name, job title, email address, and telephone number, if possible. A short sentence or notation explaining how you know each other is preferred, but this information can also be conveyed in person. Most important, always get permission from each person on your list. A surprise call from a recruiter to an ill-prepared reference never goes well and reflects poorly on you.

ONE SIZE DOESN'T FIT ALL

One of the biggest traps people fall into when looking for a job is using the same résumé for every job they apply to. This practice is a mistake! Just as different positions require different skills, different jobs require different résumés.

For example, if you're looking for a job as an administrative assistant, you'll need a résumé that highlights any experience you've had in an office environment. You'll also want to include a list of administrative skills, such as your proficiency with Microsoft Office or Adobe Acrobat Reader. In other words, a hiring manager for this type of position would most likely toss out a résumé that featured years of expertise as a line chef with no experience answering phones, using a computer, or working a copy machine.

"Regardless of the type of résumé you choose, aim to tailor your résumé to the job you are applying to," insists Alison Doyle, a reporter for the job-search website TheBalanceCareers. "While it's perfectly acceptable to use a résumé template, which you adapt to fit each job description, it's a bad idea to send the same exact résumé to multiple openings, even within the same field."

One simple way to tailor your résumé is to put a targeted mission statement at the top. Another smart option is to use what are called SEO (search engine optimization) keywords. Many companies use special software programs to scan, sort, and weed out résumés before hiring managers get involved in the process. Useful keywords or phrases not only describe your experience but they can also highlight aspects of the job included in the posting as well.

For example, a person applying for a position in customer service might use phrases such as "customer tracking system," "computer skills," and "order entry experience." Those interested

HOW TO CRAFT A STANDOUT OBJECTIVE

Not every résumé requires an objective at the top. But many career counselors say it's a helpful tool to use. Think of it like your personal mission statement. It gives recruiters a clear idea of what your talents are and what you're looking for in a job.

Just like résumés are different, objectives should be targeted, too—and they shouldn't be overly wordy. "No recruiter wants to see a large blob of text under the mission statement heading," Dixie Somer writes for ZipRecruiter's popular job-search blog. "If you want to avoid being added to the do-not-call file, make sure that you explain how you can benefit the company with your skills and experience in a succinct, clear way. Step back and look at your résumé from a distance. Ask yourself if you would read it if you were the hiring manager. If not, do some revising."

in working at a bank might have "financial accounting experience," "Microsoft Excel," "payroll," and "bookkeeping" on their résumé. A candidate hoping to work at an art gallery might include "art history" and "studio management."

Whatever the situation, using keywords that are as closely related to the specific job as possible is key. "You could have the best experience and qualifications in a whole field of candidates, and a pretty decent résumé besides, but your information will fall through the cracks if your résumé doesn't contain the right keywords," Doyle warns.

FORMATTING MATTERS

In addition to creating a targeted résumé, ensuring it's readable is crucial. Making it easy to read means no fussing with margins to include more information than is actually necessary. Don't use inconsistent fonts or formatting either—that makes the résumé look confusing. Don't include emojis anywhere, even if you think it's appropriate. This isn't Instagram. Lastly, keep an eye on the length. If you're just starting out or have only a few years of experience under your belt, keep your résumé to one page. Two-page résumés are usually reserved for more experienced applicants.

One way to make sure you're staying on target and professional is to use a preexisting template (it will also save you precious time). Microsoft Word has a bunch of options to choose from. There are also hundreds of other free or inexpensive templates online, ranging from the simple to the incredibly complex. Indeed (https://www.indeed.com/career-advice

/résumé-samples) is a helpful place to start. LiveCareer (https:// www.livecareer.com/résumé-templates) is another reputable resource but charges a small fee.

THE ULTIMATE SALES PITCH: YOUR COVER LETTER

Finally, a word about cover letters. When you're looking for work, every job application requires at least two components: a résumé and a cover letter. Without a cover letter, it's almost guaranteed that your application will be ignored.

Think of the cover letter as your elevator pitch. If you're standing in an elevator with your hiring manager, you have the length of the elevator ride to

The key to crafting a convincing elevator pitch is making it clear and concise, so make sure to do the same with your cover letter.

make a top-of-the-line impression, so you better make it count! Here are some helpful tips for crafting a slam-dunk cover letter:

- If at all possible, address your letter specifically to the person doing the hiring. If that contact's name isn't included in the job listing, try to dig that information up on LinkedIn. "Dear Hiring Manager" works as a last resort, but using the actual person's name is always preferable.
- Mention the most important information in the opening paragraph, including a short, but explicit, sentence or two about why you want to work at the company and why your skills would be a great fit for the job. Be specific about what the company does and why that matters to you to show you've done your research.
- Use a clean, uncluttered layout and short paragraphs.
- Don't change the margins so you can cram in more information. White space is important!
- Don't ramble. The cover letter is a curated presentation of who you are and what you can do, but it also highlights your writing. A long-winded cover letter doesn't project a confident image.
- If you're using one cover letter for different jobs, make sure each one is adequately modified by using different keywords. If you swap out key details like the company's name, be sure

you've done so all the way through to avoid embarrassment later on.

- Read the document through three times or more to make sure there aren't any spelling or grammatical mistakes. There's nothing that speaks louder than a typo in a job application.

Above all, your cover letter should highlight your flair for writing without reiterating every single thing in your résumé point by point. That being said, if there's something in your résumé you'd like to expand on—a specific skill or a gap in your work history, for example—feel free to do so here. When viewed as a package, your résumé and cover letter should serve as a neat, succinctly put-together snapshot of who you are and what you can bring to the table.

CHAPTER THREE

NAVIGATING THE JOB SEARCH

Here's a big myth about navigating the job search: because there are so many internet job boards, looking for work has become easier than ever before. All you have to do is search for jobs online and apply to all of the ones that interest you. Then you can sit back and wait until you get called for an interview. Right?

Unfortunately, following the online-only, wait-and-see method is an incomplete approach, not to mention unhelpful. In an interview for Goop, Lauren McGoodwin, founder and CEO of career counseling service Career Contessa, called the move a waste of time. "When you apply online only and call it a day, you might as well not apply at all," she says. "That's because there are thousands of online applications for each role and maybe just one recruiter reviewing them." McGoodwin further insists there needs to be a balance between searching online and actual in-person networking. "Networking and referrals to companies are definitely the best way to get your foot in the door," she writes.

So how do you effectively and efficiently use the internet to optimize your job search? What exactly is networking and how do you network with people you have never met before? Here are a few pointers to get you started.

THE ONLINE SEARCH

There are many ways to look for work. For one, the internet provides you with a wealth of resourceful tools literally at your fingertips. Browsing company websites, reading news articles about organizations and their corporate culture, and doing general research about your fields of interest are all easily navigable ways to add fire to your search.

In terms of looking for companies that are actually hiring, many job boards and aggregate sites not only list job postings, but also contain information about how to look for a job, which

Job boards and aggregate sites like LinkedIn, Indeed, and Glassdoor make the job search easier because they provide listings and advice all in one place.

résumé templates are best to use for specific positions, and how to pull off a superstar interview. Most of the materials posted on these sites are written or at least vetted by professional career counselors, recruiters, or human resources managers with years of experience and proven results. Examples include Indeed (https://www.indeed.com); LinkedIn (https://www.linkedin.com); Monster (https://www.monster.com); CareerBuilder (https://www.careerbuilder.com); and LinkUp (https://www.linkup.com), a clearinghouse of open positions that are otherwise posted only on company websites.

In addition, a growing number of websites feature anonymous, down-and-dirty reviews of what it's actually like to work at a company. Glassdoor (https://www.glassdoor.com/index.htm) is a website that offers not only job postings, but also helpful inside information, such as typical salaries for different positions and interview tips from people who have gone through the process. InHerSight (https://www.inhersight.com) posts honest opinions from present and former employees of what it's like to be a woman working at certain companies.

No matter which website or group of websites you choose to use, set up email alerts for the types of jobs you're looking for. That way, daily or weekly results will be sent to your inbox without you having to do the legwork each time. In some cases, such as on Indeed and LinkedIn, a section of the website allows you to upload your résumé into a database that's searchable by recruiters. LinkedIn also gives you access to dozens of industry or skill-related groups and organizations where you can network with others and share valuable information.

FIND A JOB IN A NICHE MARKET

Websites like Monster, Indeed, and LinkedIn are excellent resources when it comes to looking for work. They have a broad reach and are used by millions of recruiters and companies in the United States and around the world. But depending on what type of job you're looking for, there are also targeted sites and apps directed toward applicants searching for work in a specific field.

For example, Dice (https://www.dice.com) posts listings for jobs in the technology sector. Mediabistro (https://www.mediabistro.com) lists jobs in book publishing and other media-related professions. Idealist (https://www.idealist.org/en/?type=JOB) targets full-time, part-time, contract, or volunteer positions at nonprofit organizations. Snag (https://www.snagajob.com) posts hourly jobs and has a section for teens.

STAFFING AGENCIES AND JOB RECRUITERS

If you're starting out, changing careers, or just looking for a little help along the way, staffing agencies are another great way to land a full-time job and even find seasonal work without the full responsibility of committing to one particular company. At a staffing agency, companies pay the agency to find suitable employees for them. Therefore, it's in the staffing agency's best interest to find appropriate candidates so it can get paid.

Here's how the process works. Most staffing agencies ask for a résumé before you even get in the door. In some cases, particularly if you're in the market for temp or temp-to-hire positions, they'll have you perform tests on various programs, such as Microsoft Excel or accounting software, to demonstrate your proficiency. The recruiter will also do an interview to find out your skills and past career experiences.

Recruiters at staffing agencies can pair you with jobs that best match your skills. Some can even coach you on interview techniques or how to negotiate your salary and benefits.

Signing up with a staffing agency is usually a win-win situation. It's a recruiter's job to advocate for his or her clients. Recruiters send candidates job listings for suitable temporary, temp-to-hire, or permanent positions and help them prepare for interviews. They can also help negotiate things like salary, paid time off, and benefits. The best part about working with a staffing agency is that it's almost always free.

Similar to job boards, there are hundreds of staffing agencies across the United States. Some big firms, such as Adecco or Kelly Services, have offices in many major cities. Others, such as TEKsystems, which handles IT jobs, or Medical Solutions, which specializes in health care openings, only work with employers in certain fields. For the most part, staffing agencies are a powerful resource to keep in your job-search toolbox.

NETWORKING, NETWORKING, AND MORE NETWORKING

Signing up with a recruiter or setting up a job alert are excellent choices when navigating your job search. But sometimes the best way to land a job is to go above and beyond either of those things. That means hitting the pavement, going to career fairs or industry-related events, and stockpiling recruiters' or hiring managers' business cards in person. This practice is called networking.

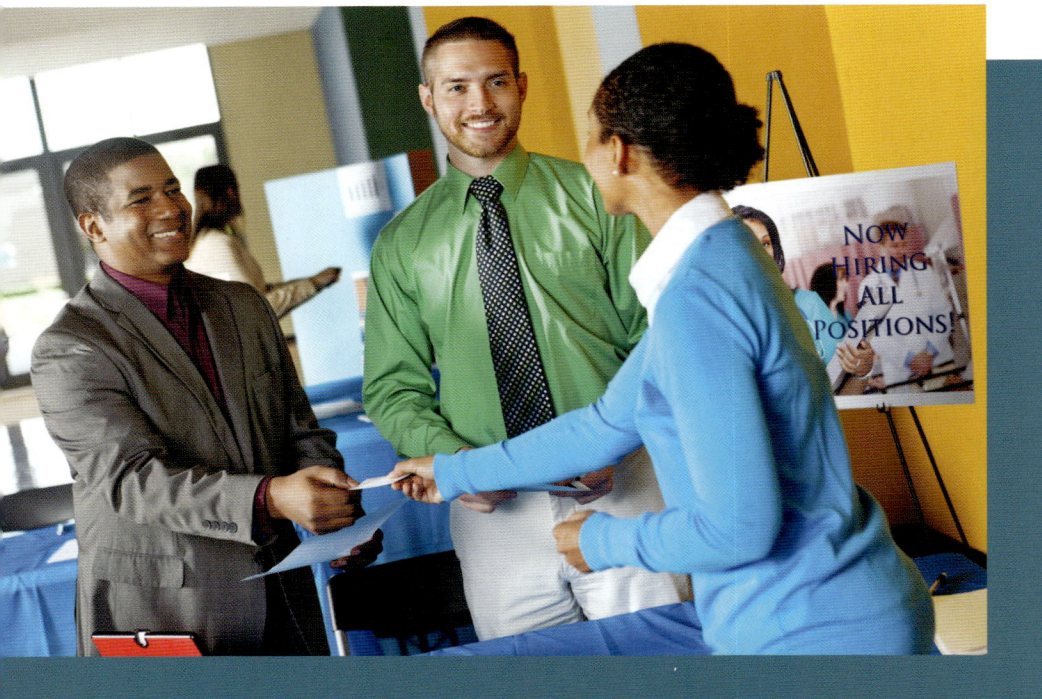

Job fairs are important networking opportunities. Dress smart, smile, and don't forget to pick up business cards from people who might be worth talking to in the future.

LEVERAGING YOUR SOCIAL MEDIA PROFILE

Social media is fun, especially when it comes to posting and sharing photos with friends. But it can also be a resourceful networking tool, especially in the research phase. Scrolling through a company's Instagram and Facebook pages or Twitter feed can give you a sense of who is working there, what issues the company cares about, and even how certain teams celebrate their successes.

On the flip side, creating a profile on LinkedIn and using it to connect with potential employers and to communicate your brand is a no-brainer when it comes to networking. Many companies will use LinkedIn, Instagram, and even Twitter to post jobs that aren't posted elsewhere. Make sure your profile is clean, professional, and G-rated at all times. "You never know who will come across your profile, so put your best foot—and best work—out there for hiring managers to find," writes reporter Franny Goldberg for Mediabistro.

Social media is fun, but it's also a powerful business tool. Use it to your advantage and create a dynamic, engaging, and responsible profile that highlights your uniqueness and potential.

One risk-free option is to set up informational interviews at companies where you'd like to work. This step gives you a chance to ask a current employee questions you might not be able to address in an actual job interview. For example, what kinds of projects do entry-level employees tend to work on? What's the hiring process like? How did this person get hired for the position, and does he or she like the job? It also puts the person with whom you're meeting at ease. They might be more candid about the company and its culture if they know you're not gunning for a specific open position.

Alumni and community associations are important resources, too—especially for people just starting out in their careers. Having something in common with a networking contact—other than work—is an easy way to break the conversational ice. Your new contact will also be more likely to remember you later on if a job opportunity comes up.

There's no denying that networking can feel icky, especially if you're shy or not used to putting yourself out there. But it's not something you can ignore in today's highly competitive job market. "Networking is an essential part of advancing your career. I often tell my own children, 'You will likely get a job through who you know rather than through your education or work experience,'" says president and CEO of the Children's Hospital of Philadelphia, Madeline Bell, in the *Huffington Post*. "These days, it's not enough to keep your head down and produce A-plus work. You need to connect with others, be vocal about your interests and career goals, and build relationships with people you might not otherwise have met."

CHAPTER FOUR

NAILING THE JOB INTERVIEW

Early on in retirement coach and author Nancy Collamer's career, she was faced with a seemingly impossible challenge. She had to staff a department store with more than 200 new employees—and she had to get it done yesterday. Never one to miss a deadline, she set a goal of interviewing twenty potential candidates a day.

After many weeks, Collamer finally got the location staffed. The process was long and arduous. But it taught her a valuable lesson about what differentiates a good job interview performance from a fantastic one.

"Here's what I learned: Most candidates are qualified. Most come to the interview prepared with answers to likely questions," Collamer writes in *Forbes* magazine. "But the candidate who uses compelling stories to demonstrate his or her value is the one who's most likely to win the job."

But how to come up with the right engaging narratives? Using advice from an interview prep book by career coach Thea Kelley called *Get That Job! The Quick and Complete*

Guide to a Winning Interview, Collamer suggests asking yourself the following three questions. She calls them the three Cs:

- **Competence:** Am I equipped with the knowledge, skills, and past experience to do this job competently?
- **Compatibility:** Am I compatible with the company's culture?
- **Chemistry:** Do I have the right chemistry to thrive at the company?

To prove you are an excellent fit for the job, the best stories to tell in an interview address the three Cs. They should also discuss a challenging situation you faced, the steps you took to solve it, and the positive outcome in the end. Kelley's book uses the easy-to-remember acronym SOAR— situation, obstacles, actions, results—to help you come up with viable options.

"When using SOAR stories, you don't just tell an employer 'I'm a good manager' or 'I'm resilient,' you show it. That feels genuine," Collamer writes. "Done well, SOAR stories help convince employers that you're likeable, competent and the best fit for the job."

But acing an interview takes more than just being a good storyteller. Like every step of the job-search process, it all starts with your prep.

STEP UP YOUR PREP

Getting called in for an interview is a stupendous achievement. But in many ways, what you do before the interview is just as important as how you act in the interview itself. To show you're the best candidate for the job, you have to know everything there is to know about the company at which you're interviewing.

First scour every page of your prospective employer's website to get a sense of who they are and how they present their brand. Then read news articles about the company, its

During each phase of the job-search process, don't forget to take copious notes. You might think your memory's foolproof, but it's better to be safe than sorry.

management, and its accomplishments, if any are available. Revisit Glassdoor and other anonymous review sites to find out interview-related tips or feedback from people who work there. You can even check out the public social media profiles of current employees to see what they're working on.

Throughout this research phase, keep a notebook and pen handy. Jot down any key observations about what you read or questions you might want to ask during the interview. Bringing up all the investigating you've done not only shows you took the time to prepare, but it also reiterates how interested you are in the position—and the company.

PREPPING PRO TIP

Researching the company where your interview is taking place is doing your due diligence. But author Carol Christen suggests taking prep one step further. She tells interview candidates to get out of their chairs and physically visit the company's location a week or so before the big day if possible, roughly around the same time as their interview (without actually going inside the office, of course). This way, they'll be more aware about what to expect.

"Where is the building entrance? Which bus line gets you there, or where can you park? If you do this kind of reconnaissance before the interview, you'll be less stressed the day of the interview. The less stressed-out you are, the more confident you appear," Christen writes in her book.

PERFECTING YOUR PITCH

Many human resources professionals say that interviewers make up their mind about a job candidate in the first thirty seconds of the interview. They spend the rest of the interview trying to come up with ways to prove or disprove their decision. With such stacked odds, it's important to make your first impression count. That means being able to ask—and answer—strategic questions.

When you're finished researching the company where you'll be interviewing and have come up with a list of follow-up questions, the next step is to prepare for all the questions an interviewer might ask you. One popular question is "Tell me about a time in which you didn't succeed in a task or situation and how you might change the result." A few more from *Inc.* are: "What are your strengths and weaknesses?", "Out of all the other candidates, why should we hire you?", and everyone's favorite, "Where do you see yourself in five years?"

In each of these situations, prepare a response that both reflects the three Cs and follows the SOAR approach. For example, a candidate answering a question about her weaknesses might say, "Early on in my previous job as an editorial assistant, I had trouble saying no. I took on too many projects and ended up working nights and weekends. It was stressful, so I started asking my boss which projects were a priority. I also began using workload management tools to help me better organize my time. Since then, my workload has stayed the same but I've completed more manuscripts on time without taking them home." This response shows that she is both self-aware and striving to continuously get better at her job, with measured success.

After you've come up with fifteen to twenty question-and-answer pairs, practice answering them out loud to make sure you sound professional. Better yet, enlist the help of family members or friends. Ask them to be objective about your responses to help you improve your delivery. Even if it feels embarrassing, the more you practice, the better you'll sound during the interview.

Before an interview, practice what you'll say out loud with a trusted friend or family member. It might feel silly at first, but you'll feel more prepared with each run-through.

PLAN YOUR WARDROBE

The other crucial part of perfecting your pitch means planning your wardrobe. Even if you consider yourself stylish, never wing it. Lay out your clothes the night before. Dress responsibly. While not every interview requires a suit, dressing to impress means looking professional. Jeans, shorts, flip-flops, or shirts with slogans of any kind are prohibited. Women should avoid very short skirts, while men should make sure their shirts and pants aren't skintight.

Acing a job interview takes poise and style. Suit jackets are a smart choice for office settings. A button-up shirt and an ironed skirt or pants work for less corporate environments.

Of course, what you wear will depend on the type of field you're interested in. For most office positions, the more professional you can be, the better you'll be perceived. If you want to add a little personal style, do so in your accessories. Avoid wearing any kind of perfume or cologne—it's distracting. Plus, your interviewer might have an allergy. Make sure your purse, bag, or briefcase is presentable and organized. Last but not least, use an iron if you have one. Wrinkled clothes not only project a disheveled image, they also imply the interview candidate is woefully overwhelmed.

GETTING IT DONE

Unless the applicant happens to be a robot, everybody gets nervous before a job interview. After all, you're trying to project a cool, confident, and collected image while also remaining calm. Aside from remembering to project why you'd be a great fit for the job, there are a few tried-and-true rules to follow in order to come out on top.

Priority number one is to be on time. If possible, be early. It'll give you time to settle your nerves and focus before the meeting takes place. Always turn off your phone before you even step foot in the building—that means don't just put it on vibrate. Mistakes happen, and there's nothing more embarrassing than your party-anthem ringtone sounding off loud and clear just as you're explaining why you want the job.

During the interview, try a bit of friendly banter before, during, and afterward (but not too much). Pay attention to your body language and make sure it implies confidence. Deliver

Let your personality shine during your job interview. Be friendly and professional. Good posture and eye contact are key. Don't forget to smile!

a firm handshake. Maintain eye contact. Sit up straight. Try not to fidget too much. An incessantly bouncy leg is a sign of anxiety and weakness.

When answering questions, actively listen to what the interviewer is saying before responding to make sure you've heard the question correctly. Don't be afraid to take a moment to collect your thoughts so they don't come out either jumbled or overly rehearsed. Play up your strengths, but be honest about your weaknesses. Whatever you do, never think of an interview as a therapy session. If possible, reframe your shortcomings and negative experiences as learning opportunities and areas for growth, rather than rehashing all the reasons why you and your previous boss didn't get along.

Some interviewers might require you to take a test to prove your competency in a certain area. Ask any pertinent questions before you begin.

If you've been asked to take any tests during or after the interview—an editorial test or copyediting test, for example—take the time to find out any pertinent information before actually beginning the exam. If the test is not administered onsite, find out when it's due. Ask what the protocol is if you have questions related to the exam and whether or not outside research is permitted.

Finally, breathe. Yes, interviewing can be taxing, especially if you really want the job. But keep in mind, if you don't do well on the first go, that's OK. There will always be another interview down the road. In the meantime, good luck. You've got this!

10 GREAT QUESTIONS
TO ASK AN INTERVIEWER

1   **Can you tell me more about the day-to-day responsibilities of this job? What would a typical day or week be like?**

2   **What do you think are the most important qualities for someone to excel in this role?**

3   **What are your expectations for this role during the first thirty days and how might that evolve over the next year or two?**

4   **Thinking back to people who've previously held this position, what differentiated the bad or mediocre employees from the ones who were really successful at it?**

5   **Are there opportunities for professional development? If so, what do those look like?**

6   **What are the biggest opportunities and challenges facing this department right now? How about the company?**

7   **How would you describe the culture of this company?**

8   **What type of people tend to really thrive at this company, and what type don't do as well?**

9   **What do you like best about working for this company?**

10   **What are the next steps in this interview process?**

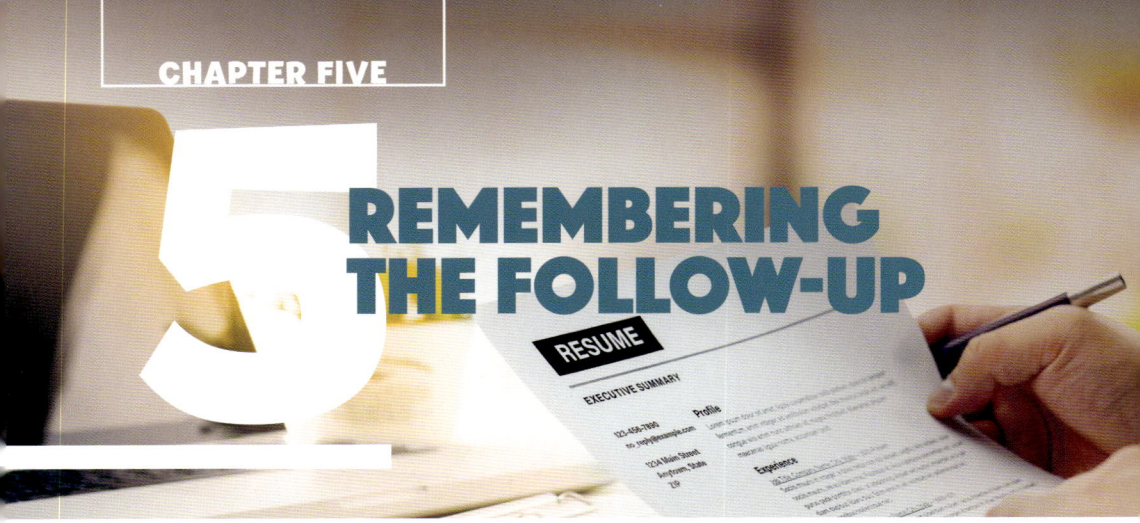

CHAPTER FIVE

5 REMEMBERING THE FOLLOW-UP

Here's a bit of bad news. Sometimes you can have a top-notch résumé, write a compelling cover letter, and nail your interview, but still not get your dream job. Yes, there might be a candidate more suitable than you for the position. But sometimes it has to do with your follow-up.

Consider this example. A reader wrote in to the career-guidance website The Muse (https://www.themuse.com) with a funny but unfortunate story. She had interviewed for a position at a nonprofit organization and really wanted the job. She emailed the executive director of the company to thank her and reiterate her interest. Because she wasn't at home, she sent the email using her phone, which turned out to be a terrible move.

"While I thought I wrote 'I can hardly contain my excitement about the possibility of working with your organization,' auto-correct changed 'excitement' to 'excrement.' It was far and away the worst auto-correct disaster I have ever had," the reader shared in the blog post.

WHAT YOU NEED TO KNOW ABOUT JOB SEARCHING

Luckily, the executive director laughed when the reader called her to apologize. But the candidate still didn't get the job. As this example shows, following up after a job interview is always smart. But it pays to be extra cautious. Knowing what to say or write—and when to say or write it—can have long-lasting consequences.

PLEASE AND THANK YOU

Your mom probably taught you that it's important to thank your aunt for the birthday gift she sent for your sweet sixteen. Similarly, it's also smart to thank interviewers for their time. Why? A thank-you note gives you the opportunity to restate points you made during your interview. It also provides the space for you to bring up points you either forgot or didn't have time to make. "A simple thank-you letter after an interview can wield considerable power and influence, and reflect very favorably on your candidacy for the position," says Peter Vogt, a senior contributing writer for Monster.

As with cover letters, there are a few strategies to writing a solid postinterview thank-you note. Before writing the note, start by outlining what you appreciated about the opportunity or learned during the interview. Then jot down some of the top skills you'd like to emphasize that best show your ability to do the job. Finally, formally write the note (email or snail mail is fine, though email is quicker and more commonplace). Keep it concise, short, and focused. Include any links to an online portfolio or personal website if necessary. Don't forget to use spell-check. Then send it within twenty-four hours of the interview. Any longer than that and it looks like you weren't enthusiastic about the job. If more than one person was involved in the meeting, send a thank-you note to each of those people as well.

Then, sit back and be patient. If the hiring manager gave a timeline of when he or she would make a decision, don't email incessantly asking about the result. If you don't hear from anyone after the allotted amount of time, it's acceptable to send a brief follow-up email. Avoid asking if a decision has been made. Instead, reiterate your interest in the job. Ask if there's any other information you can send that might provide more insight into your skills and character.

NEGOTIATION STATION

If you receive an offer after an interview, that's fantastic news! But before you accept, do a little soul-searching. Though landing a job is the end goal, it's important to make sure the position you interviewed for is a good fit before making any final decisions.

Ask yourself if the salary and benefits package are satisfactory and adequately reflect the skills you're bringing to the position. Does the work environment seem acceptable? Did the people working there seem to like their jobs? Did you jibe with your potential supervisor? All of these criteria are important to consider before accepting the offer.

After you've made your decision, you then have three options. The first two are the simplest. If you decide the job is right for you, accept right away. If you don't want the job, also

Dear [Interviewer's name],

Thank you for taking the time to speak with me about the marketing coordinator position. I enjoyed meeting you and learning more about the job.

I'm very excited about the potential opportunity to join [Company name] and am particularly interested in the details you shared about the launch campaigns for the company's new slate of brands. I'm enthusiastic about the prospect of bringing some of my project management skills and past PR experience to the table.

After our conversation, I'm confident that my background in marketing and my strong work ethic will make me an asset to your team. Please feel free to contact me for any additional information or for samples of my work. I look forward to hearing from you.

Sincerely,
[Your name]
[Phone number]
[Website URL]

This is a sample thank-you note. Make sure to send one to your interviewer. Failing to do so might give them the impression that you're not interested in the job.

communicate that to the recruiter or hiring manager as soon as possible. This way the next candidate in line can be notified.

The third option requires proceeding with caution. If you do want the job, but there are other factors to consider, such as a job offer from another company or a low salary, tell the hiring manager you need a day or two to think about it before making a decision. Find out when he or she needs to know the final answer. Then make your call— and don't keep them waiting. If you want the job but need to negotiate on something like salary, do so confidently and politely. Do some market research beforehand about what's appropriate so your request doesn't seem out of line for the job, and always be respectful.

"Dealing with salary negotiation makes many people so uncomfortable that they end up accepting the first number offered without countering. This is a mistake, since employers generally expect some negotiation in the hiring process and have built that into their offer by initially pitching a number that is lower than they can ultimately go," writes reporter Robin Madell in *U.S. News & World Report*. "The main reason employees aren't

Negotiating can be scary, especially if you're sitting across the table from your potential supervisor. But knowing your worth— and when to accept or decline a job offer—is key.

ACCEPTANCE CHECKLIST

Before accepting a job offer, there are a few details that should always be negotiated or agreed upon before making the final decision. Make sure to get the information in writing and address any outlying concerns that weren't discussed in the interview before a final agreement is approved and a contract is signed. Here's a checklist of things to find out to keep you on track:
- Job title
- Weekly hours, including how much time is acceptable to take for lunch
- Number of vacation and sick days
- Start date
- Benefits package, including health, dental, and vision coverage
- 401(k) details and whether the company matches your contribution
- Other perks, including gym membership, employee cafeteria access, public transportation or parking passes, and tuition reimbursement
- Whether working remotely is possible and, if so, how often
- Dress code

paid what they're worth isn't because they don't deserve it. It's because they don't ask."

HANDLING REJECTION

Not everyone lands the first job they apply for. In fact, most people don't. Still, as Kelly Williams Brown so wisely says, there's more than one amazing job for every person who is searching for employment. If you didn't get hired this time, use it as a learning experience to figure out how you might

Don't beat yourself up if you don't get the job. If your interviewer is open to it, ask for feedback. Sometimes a quick phone call can be illuminating.

tweak your résumé for a different outcome or upgrade your interview performance.

If you sense that the hiring manager would be open to giving you feedback, however, probing for reasons why you didn't get the job isn't a bad thing to do. Just be careful not to sound defensive. In addition, ask the interviewer if you can check in periodically to see if there are any new positions that might fit your expertise. Most important: don't let rejections discourage you. Keep applying! The more interviews you go through, the more prepared you'll feel.

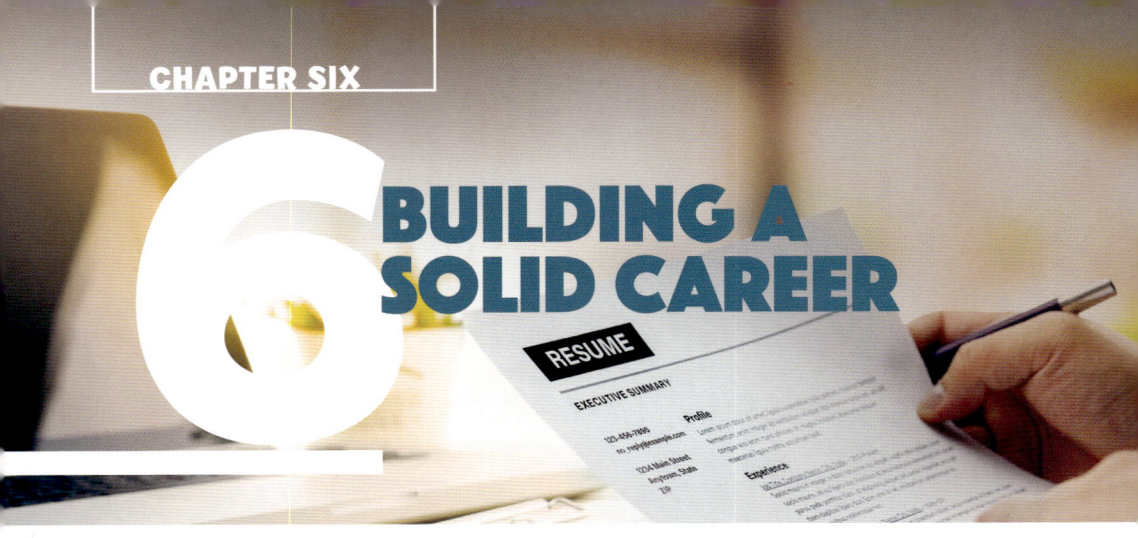

6 BUILDING A SOLID CAREER

Searching for a job can be a pain, but here's the honest truth: if you're like most people in the world, you'll have to go through the process many times throughout your life. According to the BLS, a person in the United States changes jobs an average of twelve times during his or her career. Given this rate of turnover, it's smart to know not only how to apply for jobs, but also how to act in your first job and every job thereafter.

When it comes to knowing how to behave like a pro at work, there are a few obvious no-nos. Playing solitaire nonstop, scrolling through Instagram, or shopping for clothes online when you should be working are pretty good ways to get fired, or at least seriously reprimanded. Being a good worker means projecting a capable and knowledgeable image and demonstrating a focused work ethic at all times, not just when the boss is looking.

Second, becoming the embodiment of a star employee means not just doing the right things on a day-to-day basis, but also maintaining a responsible and healthy attitude. That

Volunteering for projects is a great way for new employees to get involved. Pitch a few ideas or head up a presentation. Bosses love to see employees take initiative.

means getting enough sleep so you can perform your best on the job, eating the right foods so you feel energized and strong, and abstaining from any other activities, such as excessive alcohol use, that might interfere with your ability to meet deadlines or take on new projects.

Before beginning your first day at a new job, be sure to review these additional recommendations.

EMBRACE BEING THE NEW PERSON

It's hard to be the new person, especially at a job where you have to prove yourself on a minute-to-minute basis. Everyone else knows all the rules to follow and where the coffee maker is. It can be tricky even keeping everyone's name straight. But acclimating to the work world is not as difficult as it looks.

The best way to figure out how to act in a new office is by watching others. Pay attention to office etiquette. Do people gossip around the water cooler? Do they arrive early and leave early or arrive early and work late? Do most people eat lunch at their desks or take a break and leave during the day? Whatever the case may be, try to follow the pack, at least at the beginning. Then when you've been there enough time and have developed a trusting rapport with your supervisor and coworkers, some natural adjustments in behavior will probably be acceptable.

In terms of knowing what to wear on your first day on the job, when in doubt, overdress to impress, at least at first. Then see how everyone else outfits themselves and act accordingly. No matter what the position, some fashion options will always

Being outgoing in a new job environment may feel daunting, but everyone starts somewhere. Socializing with coworkers helps to clear your head when you feel overwhelmed with assignments.

be unacceptable, including crop tops, ripped jeans (or jeans in general, depending on the job), shorts, flip-flops, T-shirts with offensive slogans, and at some places, hats.

Perhaps most important, as a general rule, don't be afraid to ask questions. Better yet, find a friendly face and try to make that colleague your mentor for the first few weeks. He or she can help you adjust to your new circumstances as you face the challenges ahead. "Mentors are trusted advisors who help you with career decisions and advise you on steps to take to advance your career," says Terri Tierney Clark, author of *Learn, Work, Lead*. "But finding a good mentor isn't a matter of merely encountering one. You have to put forth an effort to get to know a colleague and afford him or her the opportunity to get to know you."

TAKE THE LONG-HAUL APPROACH

In any career, as in all situations in life, nothing lasts forever. Whether it's your first job or your tenth, always take a proactive approach in assessing whether you're bringing value to the company and if the work is satisfying to you. Though this shouldn't be at the top of your mind from the get-go, it's important to know how long to stay in a position—and when it's time to go.

WHAT YOU NEED TO KNOW ABOUT JOB SEARCHING

Supervisors use performance reviews to help employees celebrate their successes and get a sense for areas where they might improve. Try to take notes or get your review in writing.

One idea is to think of the first six months to a year in the job as a probationary period. This will give you enough time to get to know your colleagues, acclimate to your environment, and get used to the workload. During this probation, it's important to do your best and learn as much as you can. Then after that time is up, assess how you feel about the position. Better yet, discuss these thoughts with your supervisor during your annual performance review. If you mutually decide your role is still a good fit, set new goals for how to grow and take on new responsibilities to keep the work interesting.

If you conclude the job's not for you, that's perfectly OK. It's possible that your skills could be better used elsewhere. Or maybe you're no longer challenged by your day-to-day responsibilities and want to grow into a more senior position at a different company. These are just two of many sufficient reasons to look elsewhere for work. But what you don't want to do is quit a job without giving yourself enough time to settle in or leave because of a lack of self-confidence. Especially if it's your first job, bailing after a month because you think no one likes you or that you can't do the work is not only most likely untrue, it's also irresponsible.

"Your first job probably isn't going to be your dream job. [But] you need to start somewhere," millennial career coach Ariella Coombs tells *Teen Vogue*. "Fortunately, you don't have to get married to a job for the rest of your life. Job hopping has its upsides, too, including working with a variety of people, expanding your skill sets, and figuring out where you fit in the workplace. So, if you don't love your first job out of college,

THE EXIT INTERVIEW

At most companies, employees who quit or sometimes those who are laid off must go through an exit interview. This allows all parties involved to assess the employer-employee relationship to improve the situation in the future. Here are a few smart tips to follow:

- Voice your concerns while you're still working for the company, not during the interview. At this point, the human resources staff doesn't want to hear you ranting about how your boss was a jerk.
- Prepare for the meeting beforehand. A poised exit interview is just as important as an entrance interview.
- Show some grace by focusing on the positive experiences you had at the company.
- If you do deliver negative feedback, make it constructive by focusing on facts, not emotions.
- Don't burn bridges, and stay in touch with people who made working at the company more enjoyable. You never know what might pop up down the road.

don't sweat it." Whatever you do, when it's time to go, be sure to keep any professional contacts you've made for future references. Networking doesn't stop just because a specific job is over.

Whether you stick with your first job for one year or five years, building a strong career foundation won't happen overnight. Your profession will change as you mature over time. But every opportunity should present itself as a chance

Exit interviews can be grueling, but don't be afraid to speak your mind (in a professional manner, of course) and always try to leave on good terms.

to grow and work toward larger career goals. Now that you've learned how to master the job search and have some valuable skills under your belt, you're well on your way to a strong and hopefully gratifying career.

GLOSSARY

copyediting Reading through a book, newspaper article, or passage to make sure the spelling, grammar, and sentence structure are correct.

cover letter A letter that you send to hiring managers that describes your skills and why you want the job.

etiquette The rules governing how a person or group of people behaves.

freelancing Working for different employers or clients over a period of time without being committed to one place.

gig economy A segment of the job market in which temporary positions are the norm and organizations develop contracts with independent workers for short-term engagements instead of hiring them full time.

human resources The part of a company or organization that handles the hiring, administration, and training of employees.

insurmountable Impossible to overcome.

internship When a student or trainee works in an organization, sometimes without pay, in order to gain work experience.

keywords Important words used in a résumé or cover letter that signify certain skills or a set of experiences.

networking The action or process of interacting with others to exchange information and develop professional or social contacts.

niche A specialized portion of the job market for a

particular kind of product, service, or field.

objective A personal mission statement at the top of your résumé that describes your skills and communicates your goals.

panache Confidence in style or manner.

portfolio A physical or online collection of work that shows employers the types of projects you've worked on in the past.

rapport A close and friendly relationship in which the people or groups involved understand each other's feelings or ideas and communicate well.

recruiter A person who identifies and approaches suitable candidates employed elsewhere to fill open positions.

references People who can vouch for your skills in a certain field or area of expertise.

résumé A summary of your education, professional experience, skills, and goals laid out in one neatly organized document.

SEO (search engine optimization) The process of affecting the online visibility of a website or a web page in a search engine's unpaid results.

FOR MORE INFORMATION

Adecco Toronto
401 Bay Street, Suite 2810
Toronto, ON M5H 2Y4
Canada
(416) 214-2244
Website: https://www.adecco.ca
Facebook: @adeccocdn
Instagram: @adecco_canada
Twitter: @adeccocanada
Adecco is Canada's largest temporary and permanent
staffing agency. There are locations all across the
country and in the United States as well.

Allegis Group
7301 Parkway Drive South
Hanover, MD 21076
(800) 927-8090
Website: https://www.allegisgroup.com
Facebook: @allegisgroup
Twitter: @allegis_group
Allegis is one of the largest temporary and permanent
staffing agencies in the United States. There are
locations all across the country and around the world.

**Bureau of Labor Statistics, US
    Department of Labor (BLS)**
Postal Square Building
2 Massachusetts Avenue NE
Washington, DC 20212-0001
(202) 691-5200
Website: https://www.bls.gov; https://www.bls.gov/ooh
Twitter: @BLS_gov
BLS is the federal agency responsible for measuring labor
    market activity, working conditions, and price changes
    in the US economy. The bureau also produces the
    Occupational Outlook Handbook and dedicates a section
    of its website to information for teens and students.

CareerBuilder
200 North LaSalle Street, Suite 1100
Chicago, IL 60601
(800) 891-8880
Website: https://www.careerbuilder.com
Facebook, Twitter, and Instagram: @CareerBuilder
CareerBuilder maintains a resourceful website where users
    can search for jobs, upload a résumé, get career advice,
    and explore their career options.

Indeed, Inc.
6433 Champion Grandview Way, Building 1
Austin, TX 78750
(800) 475-4361

Website: https://www.indeed.com
Facebook and Twitter: @indeed
Instagram: @indeedworks
Indeed posts job listings and allows users to post their
    résumés for employer review.

LinkedIn
1000 West Maude Avenue
Sunnyvale, CA 94085
Website: https://www.linkedin.com
Facebook, Twitter, and Instagram: @LinkedIn
LinkedIn is a website and mobile app that allows users to
    search for job listings, research companies, and network
    with other professionals in their fields.

LiveCareer
1 Hallidie Plaza, #600
San Francisco, CA 94102
(800) 652-8430
Website: https://www.livecareer.com
Facebook, Twitter, and Instagram: @LiveCareer
LiveCareer is a job board and mobile app that also provides
    résumé templates, cover letter samples, and other
    career-related resources.

Snag
4851 Lake Brook Drive
Glen Allen, VA 23060

(804) 236-9934

Website: https://www.snagajob.com

Facebook and Instagram: @snag.co

Twitter: @snag

Snag is an online job board specifically for part-time or full-time hourly jobs. It also has a section geared specifically toward teens.

Youth Jobs Canada

#404 – 999 Canada Place

Vancouver, BC V6C 3E2

Canada

(800) 393-8060

Website: https://youthjobscanada.ca

Facebook, Twitter, and Instagram: @YouthJobsCanada

Youth Jobs Canada maintains a website for Canadian teens that provides information about volunteer work, internships, work-experience programs, and articles about the job search. The website also hosts a job board for students.

FOR FURTHER READING

Beattie, Amy. *Getting a Job in Accounting*. New York, NY: Rosen Publishing, 2017.

Chomet, Natalie. *How to Create Digital Portfolios to Apply for College and Jobs*. New York, NY: Rosen Publishing, 2018.

Christen, Carol, and Richard Nelson Bolles. *What Color Is Your Parachute? For Teens: Discover Yourself, Design Your Future, and Plan for Your Dream Job*. 3rd ed. Berkeley, CA: Ten Speed Press, 2015.

Currie, Stephen. *Teen Guide to Jobs and Taxes*. San Diego, CA: ReferencePoint Press, 2017.

Freedman, Jeri. *Step-by-Step Guide to Becoming a Leader at School & on the Job*. New York, NY: Rosen Publishing, 2015.

Furgang, Kathy. *Getting a Job in the Legal Profession*. New York, NY: Rosen Publishing, 2017.

Henneberg, Susan. *Step-by-Step Guide to Effective Job Hunting & Career Preparedness.* New York, NY: Rosen Publishing, 2015.

Kamberg, Mary-Lane. *Getting a Job in the IT Industry*. New York, NY: Rosen Publishing, 2017.

La Bella, Laura. *Getting a Job in Education*. New York, NY: Rosen Publishing, 2017.

Muchnick, Justin Ross. *Teens' Guide to College & Career Planning: Your High School Roadmap to College and Career Success.* 12th ed. Albany, NY: Peterson's, 2015.

Raymond, Tamara S. *Careering: The Pocket Guide to Exploring*

Your Future Career. New York, NY: Morgan James Publishing, 2018.

Thompson, Elissa, and Ann Byers. *Ace Your Résumé, Application, and Interview Skills*. New York, NY: Rosen Publishing, 2020.

BIBLIOGRAPHY

Bolles, Richard Nelson. *What Color Is Your Parachute? A Practical Manual for Job-Hunters and Career-Changers*. Berkeley, CA: Ten Speed Press, 2018.

Brown, Kelly Williams. *Adulting: How to Become a Grown-Up in 535 Easy(ish) Steps*. New York, NY: Grand Central, 2018.

Bureau of Labor Statistics, US Department of Labor. "Employee Tenure Summary." September 20, 2018. https://www.bls.gov/news.release/tenure.nr0.htm

Bureau of Labor Statistics, US Department of Labor. *Occupational Outlook Handbook*. "Opticians." April 12, 2019. https://www.bls.gov/ooh/healthcare/opticians -dispensing.htm.

Bureau of Labor Statistics, US Department of Labor. *Occupational Outlook Handbook*. "Optometrists." April 12, 2019. https://www.bls.gov/ooh/healthcare /optometrists.htm.

Collamer, Nancy. "The No. 1 Way to Nail a Job Interview." *Forbes*, May 2, 2017. https://www.forbes.com/sites /nextavenue/2017/05/02/the-no-1-way-to-nail-a-job -interview/#27bb3a835c29.

Doyle, Alison. "How to Write an Effective Résumé." BalanceCareers, June 21, 2018. https://www .thebalancecareers.com/job-résumés-4161923.

Gillett, Rachel, and Áine Cain. "38 Things You Should Never Include on Your Résumé." Business Insider, March 14,

2018. https://www.businessinsider.com/dont-put-these
-things-on-your-résumé-2015-75.

Goldberg, Franny. "How to Use Instagram to Find a Job."
Mediabistro. Retrieved March 11, 2019. https://www
.mediabistro.com/get-hired/job-search/instagram-job
-search.

Grasz, Jennifer. "Companies Receive More than 75 Résumés on
Average for Their Open Positions, CareerBuilder.com Survey
Finds." CareerBuilder.com. Retrieved March 11, 2019. https://
www.careerbuilder.com/share/aboutus/pressreleasesdetail.
aspx?id=pr484&sd=3%2F11%2F2009&ed=12%2F31%2F2009.

Haden, Jeff. "27 Most Common Job Interview Questions and
Answers." *Inc.*, June 20, 2016. https://www.inc.com/jeff
-haden/27-most-common-job-interview-questions-and
-answers.html.

Halpert, Julie. "Late to Launch: The Post-Collegiate Struggle."
New York Times, December 4, 2018. https://www.nytimes
.com/2018/12/04/well/family/late-to-launch-the-post
-collegiate-struggle.html.

Madell, Robin. "The Exact Words to Use When Negotiating
Salary." *U.S. News & World Report*, July 10, 2017. https://
money.usnews.com/money/blogs/outside-voices
-careers/articles/2017-07-10/the-exact-words-to-use
-when-negotiating-salary.

McGoodwin, Lauren. "How to Navigate the Job Search."
Goop. Retrieved March 11, 2019. https://goop.com
/work/how-to-navigate-the-job-search.

Rodale, Maria. "The Importance of Networking (and How to

Do It Well)." *Huffington Post*, December 6, 2017. https://
www.huffingtonpost.com/maria-rodale/the
-importance-of-network_b_9039062.html.

Somers, Dixie. "The Ugly Résumé: Top 5 Most Common
Résumé Killers." ZipRecruiter. Retrieved March 11, 2019.
https://www.ziprecruiter.com/blog/ugly-résumé-top
-résumé-killers.

Swaniker, Peter. "What Are the Pros and Cons of the Gig
Economy?" *Forbes*, January 8, 2019. https://www.forbes
.com/sites/quora/2019/01/08/what-are-the-pros-and
-cons-of-the-gig-economy.

Muse editor. "7 Crazy Interview Stories You Won't Believe
Are True." Muse. Retrieved March 11, 2019. https://www
.themuse.com/advice/7-crazy-interview-stories-you
-wont-believe-are-true.

Vogt, Peter. "The Benefits of a Thank You Note After a Job
Interview." Monster. Retrieved March 11, 2019. https://
www.monster.com/career-advice/article/power-of-a
-simple-thank-you-note.

Williams, Lynn. *Ultimate Job Search: Master the Art of Finding
Your Ideal Job, Getting an Interview and Networking.* 5th
ed. London, UK: Kogan Page Ltd., 2018.

Yate, Martin. *Knock 'em Dead: The Ultimate Job Search Guide.*
New York, NY: Adams Media, 2017.

Yuan, Jada. "1 Woman, 12 Months, 52 Places." *New York
Times*, January 4, 2019. https://www.nytimes.com
/interactive/2019/01/03/travel/52-places-to-go
-recap.html.

INDEX

ABOUT THE AUTHOR

Alexis Burling spent many years as an editor and contributor for Scholastic's preeminent classroom magazines, including *Storyworks*, *Choices*, and *SuperScience*. She has written numerous books and articles for kids and teens on a variety of topics ranging from current events and job-searching advice to biographies of famous people. Her latest books include *Financial Literacy: Managing Debt* and *Power Couples: Serena Williams and Alexis Ohanian*. Burling lives with her husband in Portland, Oregon.

PHOTO CREDITS

Cover, p. 57 PeopleImages/E+/Getty Images; pp. 5, 22, 33, 42 fizkes/Shutterstock.com; pp. 7, 17, 29, 37, 48, 56 Neomaster/Shutterstock.com; p. 9 88studio/Shutterstock.com; pp. 11, 34 Steve Debenport/E+/Getty Images; p. 13 Joe Scarnici/Getty Images; p. 14 ProStockStudio/Shutterstock.com; p. 18 Chris Hondros/Getty Images; p. 26 Stuart Jenner/Shutterstock.com; p. 30 Monkey Business Images/Shutterstock.com; p. 35 Hero Images/Getty Images; p. 39 Africa Studio/Shuterstock.com; p. 43 Ika84/iStock/Getty Images; p. 45 sturti/E+/Getty Images; p. 46 GingerKitten/Shutterstock.com; pp. 52-53 Robert Daly/Caiaimage/Getty Images; p. 55 Paul Bradbury/OJO Images/Getty Images; p. 59 Westend61/Getty Images; pp. 60-61 mentatdgt/Shutterstock.com; p. 64 Nick White and Fiona Jackson-Downes/Cultura/Getty Images.

Design and Layout: Jennifer Moy; Editor: Wendy Wong; Photo Researcher: Sherri Jackson